A Gift *for*

....

From

....

FOR THE LOVE OF CHOCOLATE

Written by Cherie Rayburn
Additional editorial development by Jane-Elyse Pryor

Design: The DesignWorks Group, www.thedesignworksgroup.com

Printed and bound in the U.S.A.

ISBN: 1-59530-113-5

Visit us on the Web at www.Hallmark.com.

BOK2063

for the love of chocolate

GIFT BOOKS
from Hallmark

CHOCOLATE'S RICH BEGINNING

No one knows what divine inspiration more than 2,000 years ago led an early inhabitant of Mesoamerica to roast a few beans from the pod of a tree deep in the misty rain forest. But it was at that moment, as the rich aroma of the roasting beans began to fill the air, that the love of chocolate was born.

Since that magic moment, the influence of chocolate has grown, taking center stage in culinary history and in the lives of countless people proud to bear the title "chocoholic."

A Sacred Tree

According to a legend of the Toltecs, an ancient civilization originating in northern Mexico, Quetzalcóatl, a king famed for his great wisdom, brought cacao seeds from the sacred lands of the first sons of the Sun. The seeds were planted, and the first cacao tree, a gift from the gods, grew in the world of mortals.

An Ancient Treat

In 2002, scientists discovered cocoa residue in pots unearthed in Belize that date to 600 B.C. That discovery is the earliest evidence of chocolate consumption.

Chocolate *Chuckles*

Man cannot live by chocolate alone,
but woman can.

Chocolate: It's not just for breakfast anymore.

Life is like a box of chocolates…
full of nuts!

Everyone has a price.
Mine is chocolate!

A BEVERAGE LIKE NO OTHER

The early Indians of Mesoamerica — particularly the Maya and Aztecs — were the world's first chocolate connoisseurs. But they consumed chocolate as a drink. Roasted cocoa beans were ground into a paste that was mixed with water into a thick, bitter drink.

Chocolate's Frothy Past

For the Maya and Aztecs, the most prized part of a chocolate beverage was the thick foam raised by pouring the liquid from one pot into another. In the 16th century, a Spanish invention called the *molinilla,* a vertically grooved stick spun back and forth between the hands, was used to raise the foam on chocolate.

Some Like It Hot

Just as today, the chocolate lovers of old liked variety. But few today would even consider tasting the combinations that the Aztecs and Maya preferred. Among their favorite chocolate flavorings — chili powder and ground black pepper!

Spain

"Las cosas claras y el chocolate espeso" is a Spanish proverb that translates "Ideas should be clear and chocolate thick." As a result of the Spanish conquest of the New World, chocolate was first introduced to Europe by way of Spain.

The Apprentice

In the late 17th century, chocolate grinding in Spain was considered a professional skill, requiring six years of apprenticeship to master. Chocolate grinders went from house to house to serve customers who preferred to have their chocolate home-ground!

A Closely Guarded Secret

Spain dominated the importing of cocoa beans and kept the pleasure of chocolate a secret from other European countries for decades. So protective of chocolate was Spain that more than 100 laws were passed to control its preparation and consumption.

CHOCOLATE IN AMERICA

The retail chocolate industry in the United States is worth
more than $13 billion per year.

———

Chocolate is America's favorite flavor.
In a recent survey, 52 percent of Americans said they like
chocolate best. The second favorite flavor is a tie between
berry flavors and vanilla (12 percent each).

———

Sixty-five percent of American chocolate
eaters prefer milk chocolate.

———

Per capita, Americans eat an
average of 11 pounds of chocolate each year.
That's 100 chocolate bars per person!

You Say "Cacao," I Say "Cocoa"

The tree from which we get the beans to make chocolate is the "cacao" (ka-kow') tree. Technically, the beans are "cacao" beans, but they are commonly known throughout the chocolate industry as "cocoa" beans.

Food of the Gods

The scientific name of the cacao tree, *Theobroma cacao,* was bestowed by Carl von Linné, a Swedish scientist and well-known chocoholic, in 1753. *Theobroma* is from the Greek language and means "food of the gods."

Where Chocolate Came From

Although theories about the origin of the word *chocolate* vary, one holds that it is a combination of the early Indian words *choco,* meaning "sound," and *atl* or *latté,* meaning "water." *Choco* is believed to indicate the sound caused by whipping up the foam on the drink before it was served.

CHOCOLATE
BY ANY OTHER NAME...

Would Taste Just as Yummy!

chocolat	French
schokolade	German
cioccolato	Italian
chocolade	Dutch
choklad	Russian
sokolata	Greek

Beware of Chiapas Chocolate!

I n an old colonial city in the Mexican state of Chiapas, the elite Spanish ladies were so addicted to chocolate that they couldn't even sit through a mass at the cathedral without it. During the service, their servants would bring them bowls of chocolate to drink.

The bishop first tried scolding the ladies for this practice, which disrupted the priests during services. But the ladies refused to give up their mid-mass chocolate. Finally, the bishop had an order attached to the door of the cathedral, excommunicating anyone who dared to eat or drink in the house of God during services. The ladies ignored the order.

A short time later, the bishop fell ill after drinking chocolate. He died eight days later, the victim of poisoning.

The Cacao Tree

Wouldn't it be great to plant a few cacao trees in the backyard and have your own homemade chocolate? Here's why that's not possible in the United States (unless you live in Hawaii).

- The cacao tree is very picky. It grows near the equator, only between latitudes 20° north and 20° south.

- It requires a constant temperature of 75° to 79°F.

- It must get in excess of 51 inches of rainfall per year.

- It is a fragile tree and cannot tolerate strong winds or bright sunlight, so it is often found nestled among taller trees.

The Pod's Hidden Treasure

All chocolate starts out as white, almond-shaped seeds, or "beans," surrounded by a sweet, juicy pulp inside a pod shaped like a small football. Pods grow directly from the trunk and large branches of the cacao tree, and each contains 30 to 40 beans.

OLD-FASHIONED CHOCOLATE CHIP COOKIES

A warm spring day is a great time to head outdoors for a picnic. So fill up the picnic basket, and don't forget the cookies!

Ingredients:

½ cup butter or margarine, softened

½ cup sugar

¼ cup firmly packed dark brown sugar

1 egg

1 teaspoon vanilla extract

1½ cups all-purpose flour

½ teaspoon baking soda

¼ teaspoon salt

1 6-oz package semisweet chocolate morsels

½ cup chopped pecans

Directions:

Cream butter or margarine. Gradually add sugars, beating until light and fluffy. Add egg and vanilla, mixing well. Combine flour, baking soda, and salt; add to creamed mixture, mixing well. Stir in chocolate morsels and pecans.

Drop dough by heaping teaspoonfuls onto ungreased cookie sheets. Bake at 350° for 10 to 12 minutes until lightly browned. Remove cookies with spatula and cool. Makes 4 dozen.

Trivia Truffles

A cup of coffee contains 50 to 175 milligrams of caffeine;
a cup of tea, 25 to 100 milligrams;
and a cup of cocoa, 0 to 25 milligrams.

The shape of chocolate
is limited only to the imagination of
the creator of the mold into which it is poured.
Originally, chocolate molds were made of wood,
then pewter, silver, copper, tin, and stainless steel.
Today, chocolate molds are made of plastic.

One chocolate chip provides enough "fuel,"
or calories, for an adult to walk 150 feet.
Thirty-five chips will take you a mile. For a hike around
the world, you'll need about 875,000 chips.

Italy

The second country in Europe to discover chocolate, Italy was introduced to the dark pleasure by Antonio Carletti upon his return from a voyage to the West Indies in 1606. Though better known today for pasta than chocolate, Italy's reputation for fine chocolate was widespread in the early 18th century, and many people traveled there from other countries to learn the Italian way of chocolate-making.

Chocolate Experiments

The idea of using chocolate as a flavor in other foods first came into popularity in northern Italy. A collection of recipes compiled by an Italian priest during the 18th century included such chocolate "delights" as fried chocolate-dipped liver and chocolate pudding with veal, marrow, and candied fruit.

A Fatal Combination

In 1705, when Rome suffered a rash of sudden deaths, Pope Clement XI ordered an investigation into the cause. The medical examiner assigned to the case concluded that the deaths were the result of bad snuff and the overuse of chocolate!

Chocolate Chuckles

My soul's had enough chicken soup.
It wants chocolate!

———

There's a theory that chocolate slows the aging process.
It may not be true, but why take the chance?

———

Chocolate is cheaper than therapy,
and you don't need an appointment.

———

In the cookies of life, good friends
are the chocolate chips.

MONEY DOES GROW ON TREES

To the Aztecs, the beans of the cacao tree were not only the source of a favorite drink but also a form of currency. Montezuma's warehouse held 960,000,000 beans. For the Aztecs, drinking chocolate was like drinking money. No wonder it was a privilege reserved for the elite!

The Going Price

A document from 1545 lists the following commodity prices among the Aztecs:

100 cocoa beans	one turkey hen
30 beans	one small rabbit
3 beans	one turkey egg
3 beans	one fresh-picked avocado
1 bean	one large tomato

Cocoa Counterfeiting

When anything, including a humble bean, is used as currency, clever people will find a way to produce counterfeits. Cocoa bean counterfeiters hid pieces of dough, wax, avocado pits, and other substances inside the hulls removed from real beans.

The Real Story

German chocolate cake did not originate in Germany. It was named after an American, Sam German. In 1852, German developed a sweet chocolate for the Baker's Chocolate Company. The company named the product "Baker's German's Sweet Chocolate." Over the years, the apostrophe and "s" were dropped from "German's," leading people to assume that the chocolate came from Germany. The first recipe for German chocolate cake, made from Baker's German Sweet Chocolate, was submitted by a Texas homemaker and published in a Dallas newspaper in 1957.

Quotable Chocophiles

Other things are just food. But chocolate's chocolate.

PATRICK SKENE CATLING

Roald Dahl, author of
Charlie and the Chocolate Factory, was inspired by
his childhood experience as a taste tester
in a candy factory.

———————

It is said that the American composer
Cole Porter got a kick out of fudge — he had nine
pounds of it shipped to him each month
from his hometown.

———————

In 1930, Ruth Wakefield,
owner of the Toll House Inn in Whitman, Massachusetts,
used broken-up bars of semisweet chocolate
to make cookies. Since then,
her recipe for Toll House Cookies has become famous
and can be found printed on every bag of Nestlé
semisweet chocolate chips.

A Chocolate Glossary

Knowing these terms will help you ace the "chocolate" category on *Jeopardy*.

CHOCOLATL: The name the early Mesoamerican Indians used for their chocolate drink.

COCOA MASS: The part of the cocoa nib that's left after the cocoa butter has been separated out.

COCOA SOLIDS: The contents of the cocoa nib, cocoa mass, and cocoa butter — mixed together.

CONCHE: A machine with rollers that heats and crushes the coarse chocolate mixture to make it smooth. The process is called "conching."

ENROBING: Covering an item, such as a cream filling, with a chocolate coating.

NIB: The kernel of the cocoa bean that's left after the shell, or hull, has been removed.

TEMPERING: The process by which chocolate is exposed to varying temperatures to give it a glossy look and smooth texture.

France

It is believed that chocolate was first brought into France in the mid-17th century by Cardinal Armand de Richelieu — as a medicine for his spleen! Today, when savoring chocolate from French manufacturers, a chocolate lover is not likely to be thinking about medicine.

Unbecoming to a Lady

When María Theresa of Spain married Louis XIV of France, she brought with her a retinue of serving women from Madrid. The women, like the queen, were all devoted chocolate drinkers. However, the queen's chocolate habit met with the king's disapproval, so she and her Spanish servants had to drink chocolate in secret. Apparently, chocolate consumption was something that proper Frenchwomen did not do — at least not in public!

Chocolate Chuckles

When all else fails, fudge it!

———

Coffee, chocolate, and men — some things
are just better rich.

———

Chocolate doesn't make the world
go round…but it certainly
makes the ride worthwhile.

———

So much chocolate, so little time…

FLUFFY CHOCOLATE MOUSSE

Try this easy recipe for a light but elegant ending to a summer brunch on the patio.

Ingredients:

A 6-ounce package of semisweet chocolate morsels

6 eggs, separated

2 teaspoons vanilla extract

Directions:

Melt chocolate in a double boiler over hot, not boiling, water. Remove from heat. With rubber spatula, rapidly stir in egg yolks all at once. Stir in vanilla.

In small bowl, with mixer at high speed, beat egg whites until stiff peaks form. With rubber spatula, gently fold egg whites into chocolate mixture. Spoon mixture into dessert dishes. Refrigerate at least 4 hours. Garnish with whipped cream. Makes 8 servings.

The Nestlé company introduced
chocolate chips in 1939. Today, the company produces
250,000 chocolate chips every day!

———————

Hershey, Pennsylvania,
home to the Hershey's Chocolate Factory,
has street names such as Cocoa Avenue
and street lamps in the shape of
Hershey's Kisses.

———————

There are three basic varieties of cocoa bean.
The richest and most renowned, Criollo, is found mainly
in Central and South America. A hardier but less flavorful
variety, the Forastero, grows best in West Africa,
and the Trinitario is a hybrid originating in Trinidad.

———————

In the 1800s, physicians reportedly prescribed chocolate
to their lovesick patients to cure their pining.

COCOA-GROWING
REGIONS *of the* WORLD

March 2000

Exhibited at "Eurochocolate 2000" in Turin, Italy,
a chocolate bar weighing 5,026 pounds was made by Elah-Dufour
United Food Companies, Ltd.

April 1996

With a diameter of 81 feet, 8 inches and an area of 5,243 square feet,
the world-record cookie was made by Cookie Time in Christchurch,
New Zealand.

April 1996

A Rotary Club in South Africa
made an Easter egg of chocolate and marshmallow
that stood 25 feet and 1 inch high. It weighed 8,968 pounds
and was supported by an internal steel frame.

A Taste to Die For

Not long after its introduction in Europe, chocolate's strong taste was discovered to be a good disguise for poison. One case of overt poisoning took place in 17th-century Spain, when a reputed "lady of quality" sought revenge on a lover who had jilted her. She held him captive in her house, where she gave him a choice: death by dagger or by poisoned chocolate. He chose the chocolate, drinking it to the last drop. He died within the hour, but not before complaining that the chocolate could have used a bit more sugar.

Quotable Chocophiles

Strength is the capacity to break a chocolate bar
into four pieces with your bare hands —
and then eat just one of the pieces.

JUDITH VIORST

The Confectioner

From Bean to Bar

How do you get from raw cocoa bean to mouthwatering chocolate bar? These ten basic steps have been followed for more than a hundred years:

1. Roast dried cocoa beans to bring out the rich chocolate flavor.

2. "Winnow" the roasted beans, or remove the outer husks.

3. What's left is the "nib," or bean kernel.

4. Crush the nibs into a coarse paste called "cocoa solids."

5. Press out the oil, or "cocoa butter."

6. After the cocoa butter is removed, what's left is called "cocoa mass."

7. Add ingredients such as sugar, milk solids (for milk chocolate), and some cocoa butter.

8. Place in a conche machine to break down the mixture into a velvety smooth chocolate liquid.

9. "Temper" the liquid, or expose it to a series of different temperatures, to give it a glossy appearance.

10. Pour into a mold — cool — enjoy!

The Military Connection

Throughout history, chocolate has played an important role in the soldier's diet.

Every day, 2,000 containers of chocolate beverage were served to the soldiers of the guard of the great Aztec emperor Montezuma II.

• When they were away fighting for the empire, Aztec soldiers carried wafers of dried chocolate, which they could mix with water for an instant energy drink.

• During World War II, much of the chocolate produced in the United States went to soldiers, who were provided three chocolate bars in each day's rations.

• Working with the Hershey Company, the American military improved the heat resistance of chocolate to withstand high temperatures during the Persian Gulf War in 1991. The resulting chocolate bars remain solid up to 140°F.

Quotable Chocophiles

At no other time has Nature concentrated
such a wealth of valuable nourishment
into such a small space as the cocoa bean.

ALEXANDER VON HUMBOLDT
(19th-century natural scientist)

The melting point of cocoa butter is
just below the temperature of the human body.
That's why chocolate literally melts in your mouth.

THE TOP 10 COUNTRIES IN CHOCOLATE CONSUMPTION

Though leading the world in cocoa
bean importation and chocolate production,
the United States is tenth among the world's
countries in per capita consumption.

1. Switzerland
2. Austria
3. Ireland
4. Great Britain
5. Norway
6. Denmark
7. Germany
8. Sweden
9. Belgium
10. United States

CONFISERIE CHOCOLAT CHOCOLAT

Switzerland

Although Switzerland discovered chocolate relatively late, since the 19th century, the country has dominated the world of chocolate. Today, Switzerland boasts such famous manufacturers as Tobler and Lindt, and the words *Swiss* and *chocolate* are inseparable in every chocoholic's vocabulary!

The Birth of Milk Chocolate

The invention of milk chocolate was the joint effort of two Swiss men: Henri Nestlé and Daniel Peter. Nestlé, founder of the world's foremost food corporation, had discovered a process for making powdered milk. Peter had the brilliant idea of combining the powdered milk with cocoa solids for a brand-new kind of chocolate. The result — the first milk chocolate bar, produced in 1879.

Quotable Chocophiles

All I really need is love,
but a little chocolate now and then doesn't hurt!

—LUCY VAN PELT *(in Peanuts by Charles M. Schulz)*

Chocolate Chuckles

A chocolate in the mouth
is worth two in the box.

Chocolate:
Here today, gone today.

Chocolate is the answer.
Who cares what the question is!

Milk chocolate…for all it's worth.

For centuries, chocolate was credited with aphrodisiac qualities. In fact, the Aztec emperor Montezuma II always drank chocolate seasoned with a dash of chili powder before visiting his harem.

A Moral Defense

In the 17th century, Johannes Franciscus Rauch, a theologian, condemned chocolate as an "inflamer of passions" and urged monks not to drink it. He even demanded that the use of chocolate be banned in all monasteries and other holy places.

Casanova's Secret

It is said that the infamous Italian lover Casanova considered chocolate more stimulating than champagne. And another infamous person, the Marquis de Sade, constantly wrote his wife from prison, requesting chocolate. No wonder the marquis grew grossly obese during his long imprisonment!

A Messy Dilemma

The Marqués de Mancera, Spanish viceroy to Peru, served chocolate, the drink of the elite, at official occasions. When a lady at one such occasion spilled chocolate on her dress, the Marqués was horrified!

Determined to avoid similar embarrassing mishaps in the future, he had made a saucer with a collar-like ring in the middle, into which a small cup could sit without slipping. His invention, dubbed the *mancerina* in his honor, soon became indispensable to every lady of high society, saving many a fancy gown from unsightly chocolate stains!

Quotable Chocophiles

It's not that chocolates are a substitute for love. Love is a substitute for chocolate. Chocolate is, let's face it, far more reliable than a man.

MIRANDA INGRAM

Dark chocolate is also called "plain chocolate" and is made of cocoa mass, cocoa butter, and sugar. Extra-bittersweet, bittersweet, and semisweet are all dark chocolates. The difference among them is the amount of sugar each contains. Extra-bittersweet has the least amount of sugar.

Milk chocolate is made of cocoa mass, cocoa butter, sugar, and milk solids.

Check the Label

High-quality chocolate contains at least 50 percent cocoa solids. (The best chocolate has 70 percent or more.) "Junk" chocolate contains only 15 percent cocoa solids. How do you know which is which? Price is one indication, but the best way to know is to check the label, where the percentage of cocoa solids should be indicated.

Can Chocolate Really Be White?

White chocolate is made of cocoa butter only and contains no cocoa mass. Only recently has the Food and Drug Administration ruled that white chocolate can legally be called chocolate. Before that, by law, it had to be labeled "white confectionery coating."

Although chocolate was born in the Americas, today, the largest percentage of cocoa beans is cultivated in the West African country of Ivory Coast. The second-greatest producer is Ghana, also in West Africa, and the third is Indonesia. Together, Ivory Coast, Ghana, and Indonesia produce more than 70 percent of the world's cocoa beans. Interestingly, however, chocolate is not a popular food in these three main cocoa-producing countries, and consumption is minimal.

———

At the health resort Bad Birnbach in Bayern, Germany, if you order a Schokolade ohne Reue, you'll be treated to a full-body chocolate soaking! The resort claims that chocolate is revitalizing to the skin, and the body retains the soft fragrance of chocolate for several hours afterward.

———

The first 3 Musketeers® bar, created in the 1930s, contained three flavors: chocolate, strawberry, and vanilla. It was changed to include only chocolate in the '40s.

CLASSIC HOT CHOCOLATE

A cup of this old-fashioned delight will warm you up on those chilly fall days.

Ingredients:

3 one-ounce squares unsweetened chocolate

$^1/_2$ cup sugar

dash of salt

1 cup water

3 cups milk

Directions:

In a saucepan, combine chocolate squares, sugar, salt, and water. Cook over low heat, stirring constantly, until chocolate melts. Slowly stir in milk, and stir until hot. Carefully pour into mugs, and top with miniature marshmallows, whipped cream, or cinnamon. Serves 4.

England

The first Englishmen to come in contact with cocoa were the pirates who preyed on Spanish cargo ships during the 16th century. But these buccaneers had no interest in the bitter-tasting beans. In fact, it is reported that in 1579, English pirates burned a shipload of cocoa beans, thinking they were sheep droppings.

Chocolate finally reached England in 1650 — about the same time that coffee from Africa and tea from Asia made their debut.

The Cadbury Empire

Cadbury, one of the largest manufacturers of chocolate today, was started by John Cadbury in 1824 in Birmingham, England. As a Quaker, John considered chocolate a good alternative to alcohol, which he held responsible for the poverty and misery of the working class of his day. The now-famous Cadbury Easter egg was first produced in 1875.

The First Box of Chocolates

Cadbury is credited with producing the first "chocolate box." It contained chocolate candies and was decorated with a painting of his daughter Jessica holding a kitten in her arms. Cadbury is also said to have produced the first Valentine's Day candy box.

Chocolate *Chuckles*

I could give up chocolate,
but I'm not a quitter!

———

Nuts just take up space where chocolate ought to be.

———

Exercise is a dirty word. Every time I hear it,
I wash my mouth out with chocolate.

———

Nobody knows the truffles I've seen!

QUALITY COUNTS

How can you tell if the chocolate you're eating is good quality?

Here are a few ways...

- Good chocolate has a smooth surface and silky sheen.

- When it is broken, it should make a crisp "snap," and the break should be clean, without shattering.

- If the chocolate crumbles or is sandy-looking, it is either too old or does not contain enough cocoa butter.

- If it bends instead of breaks, it is too old.

- If you hold the chocolate for a few seconds, it should begin to melt.

- It should have smooth, subtle aroma and taste.

How Long Does It Last?

Unlike wine or cheese, chocolate doesn't get better with age. However, dark chocolate that's been properly stored will maintain its quality at least 1½ years. The keeping time for white and milk chocolate is between six and eight months. Chocolates with fillings should be eaten within one to two weeks.

A Chocolate Surprise

After the Spanish conquest, Jesuits in the New World developed a lucrative business in exporting chocolate to Spain. In 1701, their annual shipment arrived at the Spanish port of Cádiz. On board were eight crates marked "chocolate."

When the porters tried to lift the crates, they were surprised by the enormous weight, but they managed to get them into the warehouse for inspection. Upon opening the crates, inspectors found stacks of suspiciously heavy blocks of chocolate. Upon closer examination, they discovered that the blocks were actually bars of pure gold, each coated in chocolate.

Smuggling gold from the New World was illegal, and the Jesuits denied the shipment. In the end, the gold went to the king and the chocolate to the inspectors who discovered the deception.

Cocoa beans played an important part
in early Mayan social and religious customs.
At a wedding, for example, the bride gave the
bridegroom a small, colorfully painted stool
and five cocoa beans.
In return, the groom gave his bride several new
skirts and another five cocoa beans.

————

When we think of chocolate today,
we think of it in its solid, sweetened form.
But for 90 percent of its long history,
chocolate was a beverage.

————

Each cocoa bean is nutritionally balanced,
containing 40 percent carbohydrates, 23 percent fat,
18 percent protein, and traces of riboflavin,
calcium, and iron.

PRESERVING CHOCOLATE'S FLAVOR

On those rare occasions when you don't eat all the chocolates in the box at once, keep these storage guidelines in mind to maintain that "just bought" condition:

- Store in a cool, dark place with a maximum humidity of 65 percent.
- The temperature should be 54°-64°F.
- If you must store chocolate in the refrigerator (not recommended), be sure to put it in an airtight container to avoid any moisture accumulation. Always bring refrigerated chocolate back to room temperature before opening the container.
- Remember—Chocolate doesn't like light, moisture, or varying temperatures.

What's That White Stuff?

There are actually two types of "bloom," the white powdery residue that forms on chocolate. The first is caused when the chocolate becomes too warm. This type of bloom doesn't affect the chocolate's taste.

The second type, "sugar bloom," occurs when moisture comes in contact with the chocolate. Sugar bloom won't hurt you, but it does affect the chocolate's flavor.

United States

Even before independence, the American colonists enjoyed drinking chocolate made from cocoa beans imported from the tropics. The first American chocolate factory, located in Massachusetts, was a joint venture between Dr. James Baker and John Hannon. Their product was advertised as Hannon's Best Chocolate until John Hannon was lost at sea. Afterward, the business became the Baker's Chocolate Company and is still, almost 300 years later, a well-known name in chocolate.

The Hershey Phenomenon

Called "The Henry Ford of Chocolate Makers," Milton Snavely Hershey (1857 — 1945) brought the concept of mass production to the chocolate business. His road to chocolate fame included the following milestones:

• Hershey first owned a candy business in Pennsylvania — making caramels.

• When he visited the World's Columbian Exposition in Chicago in 1893, he saw, for the first time, chocolate-making machinery in operation. After the exposition closed, he bought the machinery and began making chocolate coatings for his caramel candies.

• Later, after a tour of Europe's chocolate makers, he sold the caramel business and went full-time into chocolate making.

• The rest is delicious history!

Chocolate Chuckles

Put "Eat chocolate" at the top of your list
of things to do today.
That way, at least you'll get one thing done!

Hand over the chocolate
and no one gets hurt!

If they don't have chocolate
in heaven, I'm not going!

Forget love — I'd rather fall in chocolate.

EASY CHOCOLATE TRUFFLES

These morsels of pure delight make yummy
homemade holiday gifts for friends and neighbors.

Ingredients:

$1/2$ pound semisweet chocolate

$1/3$ cup heavy cream

$1/3$ cup unsalted butter

2 large egg yolks

Unsweetened cocoa

Directions:

Heat chocolate and cream in a double boiler. Stir until chocolate is melted. Add
butter and stir until melted. Blend in egg yolks. Remove from heat and chill until
mixture is firm. Take a teaspoonful of mixture and roll into a ball. Roll the ball
in cocoa until completely coated. Place truffles in paper bonbon cups. Chill or
freeze. Makes $2^1/2$ dozen.

November 2002

Marshall Field's of Chicago, Illinois, made a giant box of its famous Frango chocolate mints. The box weighed 3,226 pounds and contained 90,090 individual mints.

May 2003

Campers at Beals Point, a California campground,
made a s'more that weighed 1,600 pounds. It contained…

- 20,000 toasted marshmallows
- 7,000 Hershey chocolate bars
- 24,000 graham crackers

May 2002

The Northwest Fudge Factory in Ontario, Canada, created a slab of
chocolate-and-vanilla-swirl fudge that weighed 2,002 pounds.
The fudge took 86 hours to prepare and 13 people to pour into shape.
The slab measured 166 feet long, 9 inches wide, and 3 inches high.

The Baker's Girl

I n 18th-century Vienna, Anna Baltauf was a serving girl in a chocolate house. When she served chocolate to Crown Prince Dietrich, he promptly fell in love with the drink — and with the girl who brought it to him. Soon after, Anna and Dietrich married, and for a wedding gift, he had her portrait painted by the Swiss artist Jean-Etienne Liotard.

In the portrait, Anna appears as she did when Dietrich first saw her — wearing her serving clothes and carrying a chocolate service. The painting, named *La Belle Chocolatiére,* was later used as the illustration in advertisements for the American manufacturer Baker's Chocolate. Still today, a silhouette of Anna, taken from her portrait, can be found in the logo of Baker's Chocolate.

Trivia Truffles

Coffee is often served with chocolate, but it dulls the palate, so consider skipping the coffee when you want to experience the full flavor of fine chocolate.

Although chili powder and black pepper are no longer found in chocolate, modern chocolate makers are combining it with such unusual flavors as grapefruit, lavender, and saffron.

There's a new category of chocolate called "dark milk chocolate." This is milk chocolate with a higher percentage of cocoa solids for a deeper chocolate flavor.

If you have enjoyed this little book about chocolate,
we'd love to hear from you. Please send your comments to:

Book Feedback
2501 McGee, Mail Drop 215
Kansas City, MO 64141-6580

Or e-mail us at:
booknotes@hallmark.com